A Trip Throug

By Laurie Blake

LIBRARIES NI
WITHDRAWN FROM STOCK

Penguin
Random
House

Series Editor Deborah Lock
Project Editor Katy Lennon
Editor Nandini Gupta
Senior Art Editor Ann Cannings
Art Editor Yamini Panwar
Managing Editor Soma B. Chowdhury
Managing Art Editor Ahlawat Gunjan
Art Director Martin Wilson
Senior Producer, Pre-production Ben Marcus
Senior DTP Designer Neeraj Bhatia
DTP Designer Anita Yadav
Picture Researcher Sumedha Chopra

Reading Consultant Shirley Bickler

Subject Consultant Steve Parker

First published in Great Britain by
Dorling Kindersley Limited
80 Strand, London, WC2R 0RL

Copyright © 2015 Dorling Kindersley Limited
A Penguin Random House Company
15 16 17 18 19 10 9 8 7 6 5 4 3 2 1
001—271658—April/2015

All rights reserved.
Without limiting the rights under the copyright reserved above,
no part of this publication may be reproduced, stored in or
introduced into a retrieval system, or transmitted, in any form,
or by any means (electronic, mechanical, photocopying,
recording, or otherwise), without the prior written
permission of the copyright owner.
Published in Great Britain by Dorling Kindersley Limited.

A CIP catalogue record for this book
is available from the British Library
ISBN: 978-0-2411-8275-8

Printed and bound in China

The publisher would like to thank the following for their kind permission to reproduce their photographs:
(Key: a-above; b-below/bottom; c-center; f-far; l-left; r-right; t-top)
1 Corbis: Pasieka / Science Photo Library. 4 Dreamstime.com: Andrey Chmelyov (cl). 5 Dreamstime.com: Cginspiration (crb).
7 Dreamstime.com: Eldoctore. 8 Dreamstime.com: Robert Spriggs (t). 9 Corbis: Christian Thomas / fstop (b). 10 Dreamstime.com:
Andersastphoto (b/Computer monitor). Getty Images: John Eder / The Image Bank (b). 13 Corbis: Colin Anderson / Brand X (b).
16–17 Getty Images: John Eder / The Image Bank (t). 19 Dreamstime.com: Alexstar (b). 20–21 Getty Images: spanteldotru / E+ (b).
22 Dreamstime.com: Sebastian Kaulitzki (t). 25 Science Photo Library: Pixologicstudio. 31 Alamy Images: The Science Picture
Company (b). 32 Getty Images: Stocktrek Images (b). 34 Corbis: Ralph Hutchings / Visuals Unlimited (t). 37 Getty Images: Dr. Fred
Hossler / Visuals Unlimited (b). 38–39 Dreamstime.com: Bonita Cheshier (b). 41 Science Photo Library: CNRI (tl); Proff. Motta, Correr
& Nottola / University "La Sapienza", Rome (tr). 47 Getty Images: Nucleus Medical Media / NucleusMedicalArt.com (b). 48
Dreamstime.com: Skypixel (l). 50–51 Science Photo Library: Susumu Nishinaga (t). 53 Corbis: Bodo Schackow / dpa (b). 54 Corbis:
Science Picture Co. (b). 56–57 Dreamstime.com: Robert Adrian Hillman (Back). Science Photo Library: Susumu Nishinaga (c). 62
Dreamstime.com: Sebastian Kaulitzki (ca). 63 Getty Images: Springer Medizin / Science Photo Library (b). 64 Science Photo Library:
Robert Becker / Custom Medical Stock Photo (b). 69 Science Photo Library: Steve Gschmeissner (b). 71 Corbis: Sciepro / Science Photo
Library (t). 72 Dreamstime.com: Luk Cox (br). 73 Corbis: Luk Cox (tr, crb, bl). 76 Alamy Images: Thomas Born /
imageBROKER (cl). Corbis: Bettmann (bc). Getty Images: Universal Images Group (cr). 77 Corbis: Bettmann (br); Tarker (cl); Stefano
Bianchetti (bl). 79 Corbis: Ralph Hutchings / Visuals Unlimited (b). 80–81 Science Photo Library: Biophoto Associates (t). 82–83
Dreamstime.com: Bocos Benedict (b). 85 Corbis: Sciepro / Science Photo Library (r). 86–87 Dreamstime.com: Hermin Utomo (c). 89
Dreamstime.com: Ralf Kraft. 93 Science Photo Library: Animated Healthcare Ltd (b). 94–95 Getty Images: Stocktrek Images (c). 97
Getty Images: Stocktrek Images (r). 99 Science Photo Library: Martin Oeggerli (t). 100 Science Photo Library: Pixologicstudio (b).
102–103 Dorling Kindersley: Primal Pictures (c). 107 Getty Images: Ktsdesign / Science Photo Library (b). 109 Getty Images: Laguna
Design / Science Photo Library (b). 110 Getty Images: iLexx / E+ (b). 113 Science Photo Library: Sciepro (tc). 114 Fotolia: Zee (c). 120
Corbis: 3d4Medical.com (ca). 121 Alamy Images: Chris Rout / Bubbles Photolibrary (b). 122–123 Fotolia: dimdimich (c). Jacket
images: Front: Corbis: Science Picture Company (fcla). Science Picture Co. Back: Corbis: Science Picture Co. ftl. Getty Images: John Eder /
The Image Bank fcla; Stocktrek Images tr. Spine: Dorling Kindersley: Zygote Media Group.
All other images © Dorling Kindersley
For further information see: www.dkimages.com

A WORLD OF IDEAS:
SEE ALL THERE IS TO KNOW

www.dk.com

Contents

Body Mechanics

by Dan Drite and Maya Lin

From our heads to our toes, our bodies are the most complex and the most amazing machines.

No computer can match our brains for creativity and problem-solving ability.

Our eyes can focus more accurately than a video camera.

We don't just make sounds to communicate like a radio, but we can change expressions and use body language.

Our lungs don't just pump air in and out but can extract oxygen from air, too.

We're even better at adapting our movements than an 'all-terrain' vehicle. We can walk, run or climb almost anywhere.

Our digestive system is better than a food processor, as we don't just mash our food. Our intestines break it right down into useful chemicals for energy.

No toolbox is needed since we have living cells that can self-repair and heal our bodies.

We're better than fans in an oven and a fridge combined, as we can not only heat up our bodies but also cool them down.

No identical copies can be made, as our bodies are unique to each one of us, but we can pass on characteristics to our children.

Our bodies have a lifetime guarantee!

NATIONAL SCIENCE COMPETITION
CATEGORY: 8–12 YEARS

School Prize Winners

A big surprise was in store for two students at St Peter's School, as the National Science Competition named them the winners of the 8–12 year-old category last Thursday.

Dan Drite and Maya Lin, both aged ten, presented their project on the mechanics of the human body, on which they worked together to research and create at school. The two young scientists fought off stiff competition from hundreds of their peers with their intelligent and thought-provoking project.

The project explains the basic functions of the human body by comparing them to inanimate objects. The judges were very impressed by their clever understanding of how the human body works and awarded them high marks for creativity and accuracy.

Dan and Maya will be awarded their prize this Saturday at the Vesalius Scientific Research Centre. The pair have been given the opportunity to explore the inside of the human body first-hand, with the help of a tiny endoscopic camera. New technological advances have made it possible for scientists to learn even more about the body, helping them delve deeper into its inner workings and improve how we fight diseases.

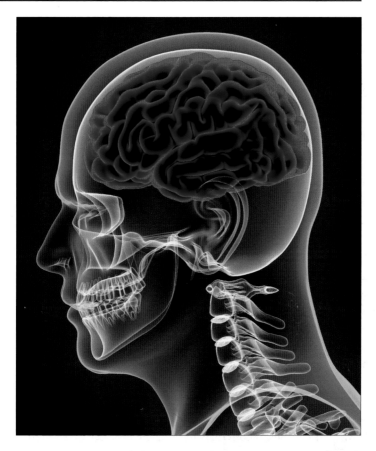

When asked how he felt about winning the competition, Dan said, "I'm so happy! I can't wait to see the research centre and learn even more about the human body!"

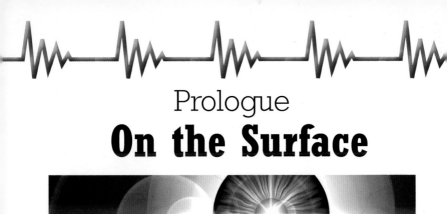

Prologue
On the Surface

"Come on, Dan. It's going to be cool!" Maya led the way through the clinic towards the research lab. "They wouldn't call it a prize if it wasn't exciting!"

Dan was less enthused. "Doctors are so serious, though. What if it's just a presentation like at school? That would be really boring...."

Maya knocked on the door to the lab, and it was opened by a tall, grinning man in a white lab coat.

"Aha!" his eyes glittered with excitement. "Are you Dan and Maya? I'm Dr Enstein, but please, call me Frank. Now, come in!

We've been waiting for you!"

Smiling, Maya nudged Dan as they entered, with Frank leading the way. Inside was a whole cluster of screens and computers, and sitting at a nearby table was a woman, smiling patiently.

"This is my assistant, Miss Mary Shelly," introduced Frank. "We'll be travelling within her today. It'll be quite an adventure!"

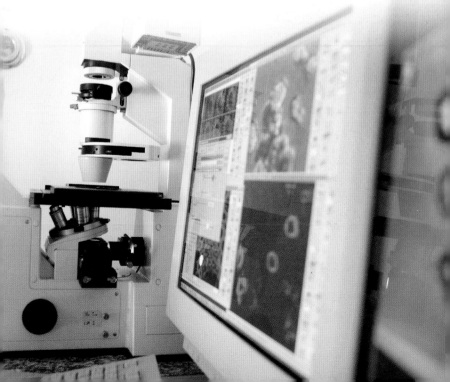

"Don't you mean with her?" asked Dan.

"Not at all!" Frank swept across to the computers, bringing up a diagram of what looked like a metal dragonfly, with cameras instead of eyes set into the sleek body. "This is the Micro-Endoscopic Remote—"

His assistant cut him off. "Frank, in English."

"Oh, sorry. Yes, Mary's right." Frank pointed to the picture. "This is an incredibly small remote-controlled camera that we'll be sending inside Mary's body, so that the pair of you get a live tour of the human body from inside."

"Wow, that's amazing!" said Maya. "But how can it fit? It looks pretty big on the picture."

Frank held up a syringe, showing them the yellow liquid inside, but neither of them could see any camera. "It's inside here," he said, "but it's microscopic, which means it's so tiny you can't even see it with the naked eye." He grinned. "I saw your project; it was very impressive. Today, you'll be able to see each of those body parts as if you were a part of them!"

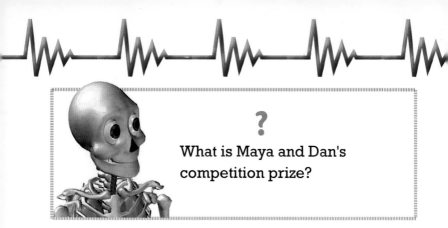

"So we'll be watching a video?" Dan sighed. "I told you it was going to be a presentation, Maya."

Frank's assistant, Mary, stood, picking up two large helmets that were on the side. "Not quite," she said. "These helmets will allow you to experience it as if you're inside, looking through the camera. Each of you will be looking through one eye, so when you turn your heads, the camera will move with you. Dr Enstein will be controlling the drone, but he'll help guide you through everything you see." She handed them each a helmet.

They sat down, and slipped the helmets over their heads.

Frank's voice was suddenly in their ears, loud and clear. "All right! Can you hear me? Are you ready to go?"

"Ready!" they cried.

The helmets switched on, and Maya and Dan looked out into their first sight of the microscopic world.

Build a Body

Here's a list of the many parts that make up the human body. Each part works with other parts to get the body's systems working together. They are all packed tightly together to fit.

Parts list

- ☑ **206** bones
- ☑ **640** muscles
- ☑ **5** litres of blood
- ☑ **32** teeth
- ☑ 1 tongue
- ☑ **5** million hairs
- ☑ **20** keratin nails
- ☑ 1 bag of skin
- ☑ 1 heart
- ☑ 2 lungs
- ☑ 2 lips
- ☑ 2 eyeballs
- ☑ 1 nose

- ☑ **2** outer earflaps
- ☑ **2** inner ears
- ☑ 1 food tube
- ☑ 1 windpipe
- ☑ 1 voice box
- ☑ 1 stomach
- ☑ 1 small intestine
- ☑ 1 large intestine
- ☑ 1 anus
- ☑ 2 kidneys
- ☑ 1 bladder
- ☑ 1 gallbladder
- ☑ 1 liver...

Position guide

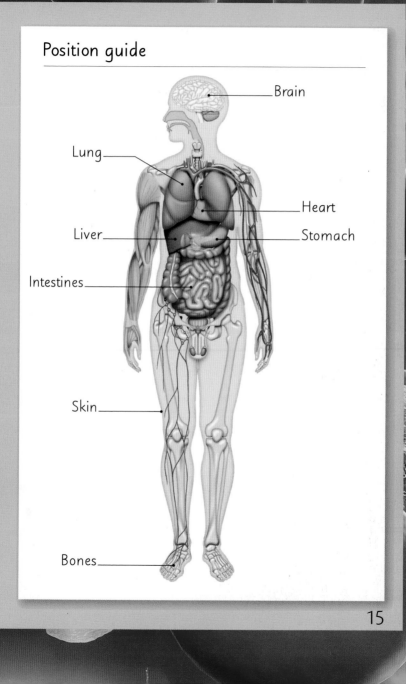

Brain

Lung

Heart

Liver

Stomach

Intestines

Skin

Bones

Camera: to film the inside of the body and relay a video straight to the scientists' helmets.

Light: to make sure that the scientists can see, since there is no light source inside the body

Scalpel: to conduct surgery within the body

The Dragonfly

This microscopic device, or drone, will be helping Dan and Maya explore Miss Shelly's body. It can be remote controlled so that they can direct it to any part of the body and it is small enough to fit into even the tightest of spaces. Here is a diagram of the useful features of the dragonfly that will help the scientists on their journey.

Wings: to help control the direction that the dragonfly is moving

Motor: to propel the drone through the body and to control the speed with which it moves

Endoscopy

An endoscopy procedure is the term used for when a doctor explores the inside of the human body. Doctors commonly use a small camera, attached to a tube, which is inserted into a natural opening in the body, for example, the mouth or nose. It can also be inserted into the body through a small surgical cut made in the skin. Endoscopes can only investigate hollow organs or cavities in the body because they are too big to fit anywhere else.

Chapter 1
Cruising the Circulatory System

Dan and Maya scanned their new surroundings, trying to find the first new and interesting part of their adventure.

"Frank, I think it's broken," Maya said. "I can't see anything; it's all just yellow!"

"Ah, the camera's working fine! Remember the syringe? You're still inside that. It's filled with blood plasma, which is the liquid part of blood. We'll be injecting you into Mary's bloodstream soon enough."

"But blood's red," Dan frowned looking at the yellow liquid surrounding them.

"This can't be blood."

"Aha, that's not quite true, but I'll explain it properly when we're inside. Are you ready? I'm going to inject you now."

"We're ready!" said Maya. "Let's go!"

There was a sudden rush as everything seemed to get sucked forward, the liquid around them pulling them along towards a huge black hole. Both Dan and Maya gasped as they were sucked into it. The other end of the tunnel flew towards them, and they were ejected out into a large tube made up of hundreds of tiny segments. All around them were large red, floating, disc-like objects rushing past, a seemingly endless stream flooding along the tube.

"Whoa!" Maya and Dan gazed around the tube, wide eyed at the spectacle. "This is incredible. Where are we?"

"You're now inside a vein!" Frank's voice was in their ears. "Each of those red disks is a blood cell, and they are the reason that blood looks red to us! When you see blood normally, the blood cells are so small that we can't see them individually, so it looks like the liquid is red."

"There must be thousands of them…," Dan said, watching the red cells in awe.

"Not even close, Dan!" Frank's grin could be heard in his voice. "There are around five million red blood cells in just one millilitre of blood, and the human body has around five litres of blood inside at any one time. So, really, you're likely to have around twenty-five trillion red blood cells travelling around your body!"

"Twenty-five trillion!" repeated Dan.

"Yes indeed! Incredible, isn't it? Should we follow them along?" The drone began to move at Frank's command, floating in among the blood cells, and was quickly washed along with them. "The body's network of veins, arteries and capillaries is known as the circulatory system, and it functions much like a conveyor belt. The red blood cells absorb oxygen that the other cells need and pass it along."

"There are more than red cells in here, though," Maya said, watching larger white cells float past them. "What do they do?"

"Ah, those are white blood cells! Simple names, hmm? They're like the police of your body. They patrol the bloodstream looking for anything that shouldn't belong or could make you sick, and then they eat them!"

Maya watched one of the white blood cells bulge its way through the others.

"That's scary. Will they try to eat us?"

Frank didn't sound worried. "If we're careful, they shouldn't notice us, since we're not a threat to Mary's body… but let's hope not. Hey! You're about to go through the heart. I'll stop so you can get a good look."

They watched as the tube opened out into a huge chamber, which repeatedly compressed and expanded, sending the blood rushing up into the huge pipe below them. The heart seemed gigantic, but Frank explained to them that what they were looking at was only half of it. "This side pumps blood into the lungs to collect oxygen, while the other side pumps it out again and through the body. The heart does this one, single function, but it's one of the most important organs in the entire body!"

"So this is what it looks like when I can feel it beating." Dan watched it squeeze the blood down the tube and refill, over and over. "It beats even faster when I'm running, so does that mean it sends blood around even faster then?"

"That's right, so it can get the blood to where it's needed very quickly. The circulatory system adjusts itself in many ways depending on how you're feeling or what you're doing so that you get just what you need at the rate you need it. It's very precise."

Maya looked down at the tube below them. "So we'll be going to the lungs next, right? I'd really like to see the lungs."

"Well, of course! It's the only way out of here now." Frank began hovering the drone up into the blood as more began to fill the heart chamber. "Hold on tight, we're about to get pumped through!"

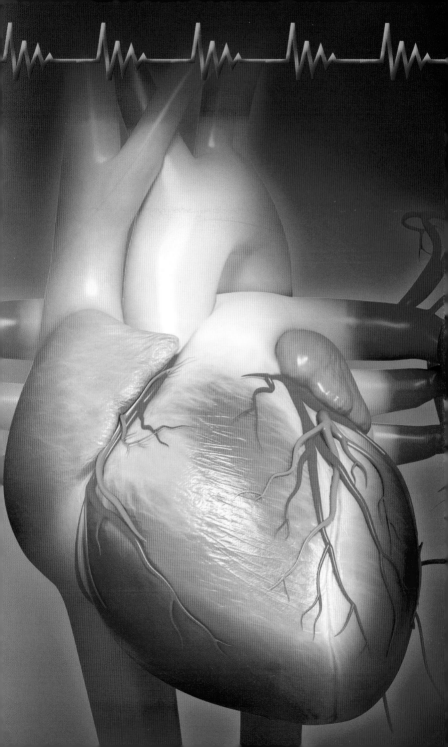

Blood Cell
QUICK FACTS

Red blood cells have a life span of 120 days. Two million new red blood cells are made by bone marrow every second.

Blood makes up about 7 per cent of your body's weight.

During its life, a red blood cell will travel over 480 km (300 miles) and go through the heart 170,000 times. That's about one trip through the heart every minute.

A pinhead-sized drop of blood contains 5 million red blood cells, 7,000 white blood cells and 300,000 platelets.

Red blood cells contain haemoglobin, a red-coloured protein that carries oxygen. A single cell contains 250 million haemoglobin molecules.

500 ml (1 pint) of donated blood can save up to three lives.

Blood cannot be manufactured – it can only come from generous donors.

Blood plasma transports dissolved substances around the body. These include nutrients, waste products and hormones.

It would take 1,200,000 mosquitoes, each sucking once, to completely drain the average human body of blood.

There are around 96,560 km (60,000 miles) of blood vessels in an adult human body. That's enough to stretch around the world twice!

The heart can continue to beat when separated from the body, as long as it has a supply of oxygen.

27

Pump it **Up**!

This diagram shows the heart – where blood comes from and where it is pumped to.

Superior vena cava: transports blood low in oxygen from the upper body

Aorta: carries blood full of oxygen to all parts of the body

Pulmonary artery: takes blood to the lungs to be filled with oxygen

Left atrium: receives blood filled with oxygen

Pulmonary veins: carry blood filled with oxygen from the lungs

Right atrium: receives blood low in oxygen

Inferior vena cava: carries blood low in oxygen from the abdomen and legs

Right ventricle: pumps blood to the lungs

Left ventricle: pumps blood filled with oxygen to the body via the aorta

What happens during a heartbeat:

The human heart works hard to pump blood to all parts of the body. Each heartbeat is made up of precisely timed muscle contractions that squeeze blood in and out of the heart's chambers.

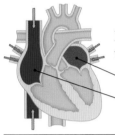

1 The heart's muscular wall is relaxed as blood from the lungs and body flows into the left and right atria.

Left atrium fills with blood full of oxygen

Right atrium fills with blood low in oxygen

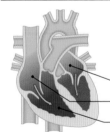

2 The left and right atria contract together, forcing blood through the valves and into the ventricles.

Atria muscles contract

Valves between the atria and ventricles open

Ventricles fill with blood

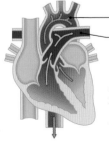

Blood pumped to the body

Blood pumped to the lungs

3 The two ventricles contract together, pushing blood to the lungs and body. Valves prevent blood from moving in the wrong direction.

Chapter 2
Riding the Respiratory System

As Mary's heart beat, the drone shot up through the pipe and into a complex web of smaller tubes. The blood ahead of them shot off in different directions as if they all knew their way. Frank didn't seem to be following any particular route, and many of the pipes all looked the same. The maze appeared to be endless.

"Are we going to see the lungs themselves?" asked Maya. "These are still arteries…."

"Well, it's here that the blood is filled with

oxygen." They could hear the surprise in Frank's voice. "But if that's not interesting enough, then we could venture inside the lungs themselves. The blood is just the easiest way to get around. I'm sure we can take a detour for you."

Frank brought the drone to a stop by the wall of the artery, highlighting a selection of much smaller, pale cells dotted throughout the blood, drifting aimlessly along with everything else. "Do you see those? Those are called platelets. Any idea what they do?"

Maya and Dan shook their heads.

"They help stop bleeding. They keep the blood in here. And since we're leaving, you'll get to see them in action!"

Frank sounded particularly excited, chuckling as a small arm extended from the drone and cut a hole in the wall of the tube. Immediately, the platelets around them began moving towards them, and as they got closer, tiny tendrils began to grow out from them, reaching out towards the drone.

"Go Frank, get us out! They're going to get us!" cried Dan, as Maya put her arms up to shield herself. The drone backed out of the artery, just as the platelets reached the hole. Their tendrils grabbed onto the edges of the tear, attaching themselves to one another until they completely sealed it off.

Frank laughed, floating the drone away from the artery so they could see the rest of the network. "They're harmless! Whenever you get a cut, the platelets join together in the thousands and seal it off completely. Ingenious, isn't it?"

"Well, you could have told us!" Dan complained. "We thought they were going to eat us for cutting the hole."

"Wait, Dan, look!" Maya exclaimed. "Look around. This… this is amazing!"

They gazed around the lung. It was a great space far bigger than the heart, but filled with a huge spread of treelike spindles, criss-crossing throughout the entire lung. Twisted around each branch were the blood vessels they had been in, and Maya and Dan realised why there had been so many different offshoots. There was just so much space to cover.

"This," announced Frank, "is the bronchial tree!" They could almost sense him do a flourish with the introduction. "It's really something, isn't it? When Mary breathes in, each branch fills with air so that the blood cells can absorb oxygen and carry it around the body. There's another bronchus just like this one in the other lung. Most of the body's oxygen is used up by its organs." He let them take in the sight of the vast tree. "What made you so interested in the lungs, Maya?"

"Oh, my little brother has asthma," she said, "so I thought maybe if I learnt about the lungs, I'd know why he finds it hard to breathe sometimes."

"Aha! Well, you're right! Let's go inside the bronchial tree and I'll show you."

He weaved the drone through the many branches, ducking towards one of the larger stems. Once again the drone made a tiny hole to slip through, and they found themselves inside, surrounded by tunnels in all directions. A tremendous wind buffeted them, and Frank pressed the drone to the side before they were blown deeper into the maze of tubes.

"Whoa, we need to be careful in here!" Frank said. "That was Mary breathing in. Since we're so small, just a breath could be like a hurricane to us."

"Is that why it's so empty in here?" said Dan, peering around. "There aren't any cells moving around."

"Ah, no, indeed! Inside here is just for air, and the body wants to keep it as clear as possible so that we can breathe. You don't want any cells getting in the way. But that's exactly the problem with asthma."

Frank took the drone higher up the bronchus. "When we breathe in, we pull a lot more than just air into us. Dust, bacteria and other microscopic things get sucked down here. That's where those white blood cells come in, making sure none of them survive in the blood."

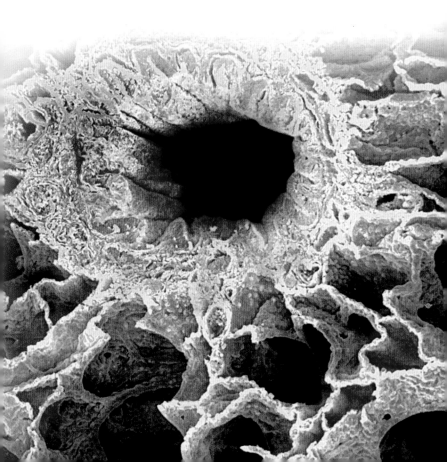

The drone rose higher into an even larger section, with fewer offshoot tubes. Dan gazed around it. "This place is much bigger! Is this still the bronchus?"

"Yes indeed!" Frank settled the drone near the wall. "It's called the main bronchus. When someone has asthma, they're allergic to something microscopic in the air. When they breathe it in, the body realises how dangerous it is and fights to keep it out. But unfortunately it does this by squeezing shut these windpipes, which makes it much harder to breathe clearly."

Maya nodded. "I see. So my brother's body is protecting him from whatever he's allergic to?"

"Exactly! Your body will always try to protect you, even if you don't know what it's doing, or why."

Suddenly the drone began to shake, and a great wind rushed its way up behind them, pushing them farther up the tube, faster and faster.

"Oh, I lost track of time! Mary's breathing out!" Frank exclaimed, and the wind caught the drone completely, and they were all rushed up, higher and higher through the throat. "Hold on! This is going to be a bumpy ride!"

Respiratory System

Breathing is an automatic process – we don't really think about doing it. Yet it is vital to our survival. Our body cells need a continual supply of oxygen to work. The air around us contains this oxygen.

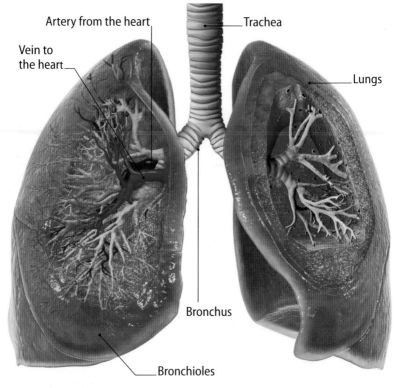

Artery from the heart

Vein to the heart

Trachea

Lungs

Bronchus

Bronchioles

Every incoming breath brings a new supply of oxygen deep into our lungs. Our body processes produce carbon dioxide. Every outgoing breath removes this.

Down the airways,

past the air cleaners,

branching off and

into the air bags

for the gas exchange.

Wow!

In your lifetime, you're likely to breathe out enough air to inflate 138 hot air balloons.

Take a Deep Breath!

STRIKE A CHORD SINGING SCHOOL

Welcome, boys and girls, to your first vocal training session with me, Ms Harmony. Today we are going to learn how to control our breath in order to make the most of our beautiful singing voices!

Breath control is the most important part of singing – it allows us to sing through long phrases and also control the volume and pitch of our voices. In order to get air into our lungs, a muscle called the diaphragm (which is located just below the ribcage) contracts to increase space in the chest cavity. This space can then be filled with air. In order to exhale, the diaphragm relaxes and this pushes air back out of the lungs. As air is on its way out of the body, it has to pass the vocal cords. These vibrate and create sound.

Let's try these simple breathing exercises to see how well you can master the art of breathing!

1 Lie on the floor on your back and put a book on your stomach. Breathe in and out slowly. You should see the book rising and falling as you breathe. You need to concentrate on relaxing your tummy muscles when you breathe in and then tightening them in order to push out as much air as possible.

2 Breathe in for 4 seconds, hold your breath for 4 seconds, and then breathe out for 4 seconds. Once you can do this with ease, slowly increase the time by one second and then keep going until you can reach 10 seconds. This exercise will help you control the movements of your diaphragm.

3 Take a deep breath and when you exhale make a hissing sound. Keep this sound going for as long as you can. Keep practising this and try to keep the noise going for a little bit longer each time. Try to make sure that the hissing is consistent, so not louder at the beginning and quieter at the end. You are aiming for a smooth and even sound.

Breathing Investigation

An experiment to test the effects of exercise on breathing.

You will need:

2 people

stopwatch

paper and pencil

skipping rope

Hypothesis

A person's breathing will become faster with exercise.

Method

One person uses the stopwatch to time a minute for each activity and count the number of breaths. One breath is breathing in and then out again.

The other person does each of the following activities for one minute. Make sure that breathing becomes normal again before starting the next activity.

Results

Draw a chart like this and record the number of breaths taken during each activity.

	Name	Name
Sitting		
Walking in place		
Running in place		
Jumping		
Skipping		

Conclusion

The more active the exercise, the harder and faster a person breathes.

Explanation

Most people breathe in about 10–20 times each minute. However, during an activity, the busy muscles need more oxygen, so we have to breathe harder and faster to take in more oxygen.

Chapter 3
Diving Down the Digestive System

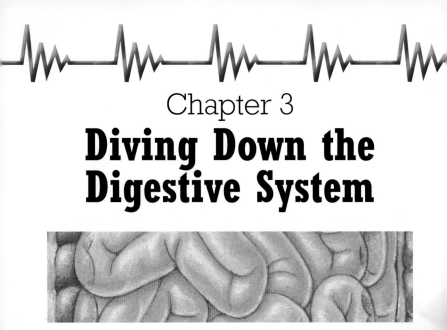

Maya and Dan couldn't see much until the whirling stopped. They found themselves pressed against a large bulb hanging down from the ceiling of the area they were in. The wind roared around them, continuing on past them and out. As they looked around, they realised that they were in the mouth.

"Whoah! Those are teeth!" Dan gazed up at the molars jutting down at them from above. "What are we doing in the mouth, Frank?"

"We're trying not to get puffed out. The uvula was the only thing to stop us."

"Uvula? I've never even heard of that!"

"Ooh, I know!" Maya cried. "It's that wiggly bit in the back of the throat! You can see it in the mirror when you open your mouth really wide."

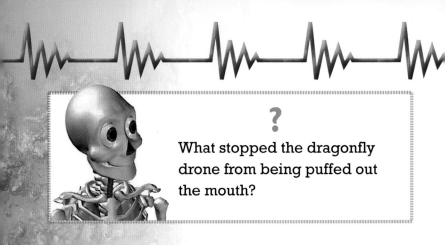

"Yes," Frank sounded distracted, "but it's not going to help when Mary breathes in again, since we don't want to get blown down her windpipe. The only thing that can stop us from going the wrong way is the epiglottis – a piece of tissue that keeps the air going into the air pipe and food into the food pipe."

Wind started to rush back into the mouth as Mary began to breathe in. Frank prepared to move the drone out of harm's way.

"Now!" Frank launched the drone off the fleshy bulb and down Mary's throat, sliding down in a wash of saliva and being guided down Mary's food pipe by her epiglottis.

"There, that's better," he said. "If we'd been sucked back into the lungs, we might've been crushed by the force. This is much safer. Think of it like a waterslide!"

"It's gross! And besides, I don't think I want to splash into that!" cried Maya, as they shot out of the tunnel, and found themselves plummeting towards a large lake of hissing, bubbling, acidic juice.

"Oh dear. Not quite like a waterslide then," said Frank, struggling to pull the drone out of its dive. "Well, at least you'll learn how digestion works!"

"I think there are better ways of learning than actually getting digested!" protested Dan, as the drone crashed into a pile of brown, sticky goo stuck to the wall, stopping them at last. "Urgh, what is this stuff?"

"Just a tiny bit of food stuck to the wall," Frank said. "Probably left over from when Mary last ate."

"Yuck!" exclaimed Maya.

"Better that than being boiled up with the rest of it!"

Maya looked up at the way they'd come, but a muscle had closed up over it, blocking them in. "Well, we can't get back out, so what are we going to do?"

"Hmm. The gastric juice is really quite high, so the mushed food should be nearly ready to be washed down."

Frank turned the drone to look around. "All we need to do is put something in and the juice will break it down, and then we can continue."

"Like that bit of food?" Maya asked.

"Ah! I didn't even think of that! Perfect!" Frank swung the drone around and began to nudge the pile of goo into the juice. "Once this breaks down, the stomach will flush the remains into the intestines so the nutrients from the food can be absorbed. We'll follow it down before the stomach closes, and re-enter the bloodstream again. We should be safe there."

The goo slopped off the wall and fell into the acidic mix, fizzling away until it had almost dissolved. As they watched, the gastric juice began to lower, and Frank flew the drone down after it. The mushed food flushed away down a hole at the bottom of the stomach, rushing into the intestines, with Frank flying them quickly after it.

"Look out, it's starting to close!" Dan flinched back as the muscle around the hole began to contract, but Frank pushed the drone to go faster.

"We'll make it!"

They shot through the last, tiny bit of space. The muscle squeezed tightly closed behind them, and they all breathed a collective sigh of relief.

"That was too close…," sighed Maya.

Dan sank back into his chair. "I thought we were going to crash for sure!"

"You kids!" Frank laughed. "Where's your

spirit of adventure? Look, we're inside the intestines now. I told you we'd get out of there. We'll be back in the blood in no time, safe and sound."

"How will you know where a vein is?" Maya looked all around. "This place is just a big tube!"

"Not at all, Maya." Frank lifted them up towards the top, closer to the walls. "If you look, you'll see lots of feelers all sticking out of the wall. They're huge to us, but they cover the entire small intestine. As food that's been broken down by the acid passes through here, these feelers absorb the nutrients out of it and pass it directly to the blood – each one is connected to the bloodstream!"

"If all the nutrients are sucked out here," Dan asked, "what's the point of the large intestine?"

"Well, there's often a lot of food, so it gets mushed down into smaller pieces by muscles, before being excreted."

Dan paused. "Excreted? What's that?"

"Oh. Well, you see, after the intestines it goes straight to the rectum."

"You mean your bottom?" Dan giggled.

"Come on, Frank!" said Maya quickly. "Let's get back into the bloodstream!"

"So that means…," Dan began, "all that food ends up as—"

"I said, let's go!"

?

How will the drone get out of the intestines?

Stomach Acid Analysis

Researcher Di Villi interviews Professor Py Sphincter in his lab about the inner workings of the stomach.

What are we looking at under the microscope?

You are looking at the microscopic view of the stomach's lining. It shows openings to some glands. When food enters the stomach, the glands release **gastric juice**. The movements of the stomach's muscular wall churn the food and juice around.

What are the components of gastric juice?

It's a strong mix! There are enzymes called **proteases** and an acid mainly composed of **hydrochloric acid**, potassium and sodium.

What do the proteases do?

They are bond-breakers! The **proteases** break down (digest) all the proteins in the food. They break the chemical bonds in proteins to free the chemicals (amino acids) needed by the body. **Proteases** work best in acid. After three to four hours, the food and juice becomes a creamy liquid.

Isn't hydrochloric acid very strong?

Yes, that's right. The **hydrochloric acid** is stronger than lemon juice. Outside the body, it can strip paint or eat right through a piece of wood. Inside your stomach, it makes conditions so harsh that dangerous bacteria on the food can't survive.

Why doesn't the acid eat the stomach too?

It's protected! The stomach is lined with mucus and some other glands release sodium bicarbonate. Bicarbonate is an alkali, which balances the acid, producing harmless salt and water.

Do you have any final Wow! facts?

Here's my best one: during an average lifetime, a person can eat and digest up to 50 tonnes of food and release about 2–3 litres of gastric juice every day.

The Journey of Food····┐

Join your food guide on an amazing two-day trip through the human digestive system. This rollercoaster tour will let you experience first-hand what happens to food after it has been eaten. An absorbing travel experience for any morsel!

Terms and conditions

Journey times may vary (between 20 and 48 hours) depending on the type of food being digested.

ITINERARY

00:00:00
Arrival in the mouth where food will be gnashed by teeth and mushed up with saliva.

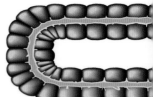

00:00:30
A wild rollercoaster ride down the contracting esophagus, arriving in the stomach.

00:00:40
Food spends up to four hours, churning in the stomach, among the gastric juices.

04:00:00
In a creamy relaxed state, food enters the small intestine and is squeezed along by muscles. The most nutritious parts will swirl around the tiny villi and be transferred into the blood system.

09:00:00
The watery, indigestible waste that remains on the tour will enter the large intestine. Meet the friendly bacteria that dry food out and turn it brown. You'll be overwhelmed by the smelly experience.

45:00:00
As semisolid faeces, food arrives in the rectum, where a muscle triggered by the brain makes the final push.

The Scoop on **Poo!**

All animals **poo**, but waste products differ depending on what the animal eats.

Herring gull

Diet: gulls hunt for fish and other sea creatures and also eat eggs, worms and other small mammals.

Shape of dung: herring gulls' faeces is usually excreted as liquid, but they have a delicate digestive system so they need to regurgitate, or 'throw up', food that they are unable to digest.

Interesting fact: some people believe that it is good luck to be pooed on by a bird.

Rabbit

Diet: all rabbits are herbivores and survive on grass, flowers and weeds.

Shape of dung: rabbits have two types of droppings: some are small hard pellets, and others are soft black pellets.

Interesting fact: rabbits struggle to digest all of the plants that they eat so they eat their soft pellets, digesting their food further and taking in extra nutrients.

Here is an idea of what different animal dung is like – from very big animals to very small ones.

Elephant

Diet: elephants are herbivores and their diet consists of grass, leaves, bark, twigs and fruit.

Shape of dung: elephant dung is large and round and full of undigested grass.

Interesting fact: elephant dung can be used to make paper because it is very fibrous. This is a great alternative to paper made from trees because it is a natural and plentiful resource.

Human

Diet: most humans have a varied diet that needs to include a healthy balance of carbohydrates, fats, proteins, vitamins, minerals, fibre and water.

Shape of dung: human faeces vary from person to person since everyone has a different diet.

Interesting fact: humans create a new stomach lining every three to four days. If they didn't, the strong acids their stomach uses to digest food would also digest their stomach.

Chapter 4
Intercepted by the Immune System

The platelets sealed up the hole behind them as they rejoined the blood, flowing along with all the red blood cells once again. The vein they were travelling down began to split off. Blood flowed off in different directions until the vein they were in opened up into a much larger area. It was filled with a strange collection of parts, each seeming to do a different job as the blood flowed through and around them.

"Ah, yes! This is the liver! This is where all those nutrients get taken from the blood and properly processed! It's quite a sight, don't you think?" said Frank.

"I'm… not even sure what we're looking at," Dan said. "What are all these things doing?"

"Well, the liver is like a huge factory! It takes the nutrients, turns them into anything the body needs, and then sends them to the right places. It also cleans and filters the blood, but we want to avoid that if we can."

"Why?" asked Maya. "We probably need a bit of a wash after everything we just went through…."

"Well, yes," Frank said, "but it's filtering the blood for anything that shouldn't be in here. Plenty of viruses and bacteria try to get into the blood through food, so the liver cleans them out. Even if they do get through those cleaning fronds, it will alert all the white blood cells in the area."

Maya paled. "And they'll try to eat us."

"Yes, not exactly the best way to end the journey!" replied Frank.

They continued through, watching as the blood passed through the fronds and frills like fish through seaweed. Frank darted between them, keeping away from each one as they followed the stream. The section parted, and some of the blood they were travelling with rushed off in a different direction. The drone stayed in the main tube, moving into the next area.

"Hey, have we gone around in a circle?" asked Dan. "This next bit looks exactly the same as the last bit!"

"Oh, no!" said Frank. "This is a new bit. It's just that the liver is made up of many different sections, called lobules, which make sure no blood cell is missed. They filter it again and again, and collect all of the nutrients. We've still got several to go!"

They dodged through another section, weaving along, trying carefully not to get caught by the fronds. As Frank swerved away from one reaching out to engulf them, the drone accidentally bumped into a white blood cell, bouncing off it and causing it to float away from them. It stopped a second later, unmoving, ignoring the flow of cells around it. As Maya, Dan and Frank watched, others began to do the same – stationary white cells in the rush of red.

"Why have they stopped?" said Maya, unnerved. "I don't like this. It's creepy."

Frank sped up the drone, so that it moved along faster than the flow of cells.

"Aha, just ah, stay calm, I'm sure it's fine…," he said, but the white blood cells moved with them, staying alongside. "I think it might be best if we sped up a bit more and skipped a little sightseeing, if that's all right?"

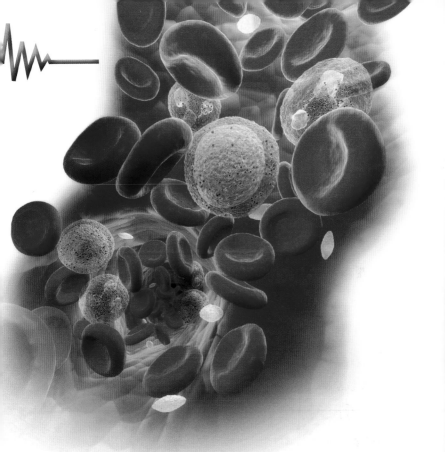

"Yes!" Maya and Dan chorused. "Get us out of here! They're getting closer!"

Frank quickened the drone even more, pushing it as fast as it could go. They raced through the vein to try to outrun their attackers. Dan and Maya looked back, but the white blood cells were catching up quickly.

"They're going to eat us!" Maya cried, looking away. "What are we going to do, Frank?"

"It's all right! I'll think of something!" he said, but up ahead were more of them, turning to chase the drone. "You know, on the bright side, if we were an infection you can see why Mary would be able to fight off the invading bacteria."

"It's not a bright side when her body thinks we're the bacteria," Dan said. "There are too many of them. They'll catch us for sure!"

"We can't go any faster," Frank said as he dodged one that was close enough to open up, ready to engulf the drone within it. "They'll surround us soon; we can't dodge all of them!"

"Quick! What about that?" Dan said, pointing out a much smaller blood vessel. "If we get in there, they can't surround us."

"Ah! That's a capillary! Perfect!"

Frank swooped into the opening, rushing down into the tiny tube. "This only has room for one cell at a time, so they'll need to follow us single file."

They followed the tube down, only to find more blood cells flowing down the vessel ahead. Frank slowed to avoid crashing into the platelet in front before trying to push past the traffic.

"They're catching up again!" Maya said. The white cells bulged along behind them. "We've got to get past them!"

"We can't! The gap is too small." Exasperation was in Frank's voice. "We're… we're trapped."

"That's a platelet, though," Dan said.

"Yes, I know! I can't get past it!"

"But we can use it," Dan insisted. "We can cut out of here and it'll close it up."

"They're nearly here!" Maya cried.

"All right, let's do it!" Frank spun the drone around, cutting a tiny hole in the side of the

vessel wall. Immediately the platelet sprang to life, rushing to fix the gap as they drove through. As they looked back, they saw the white blood cells swarm around the hole, just as the platelet fused it shut.

"We're through... we made it...," Maya panted, "but... where are we?"

Disease Destroyers

Help! The human body is being attacked! Have a look at the white blood cells below. Each cell has its own special function to keep the body safe from germs and infections. Identify the danger and choose the right one to save the body.

**Join the Immunity Army!
It's bacteria-bashing time!**

The Scavengers

Monocyte

Monocytes patrol the tissues in the body in search of intruders. They are able to kill infected host cells that bacteria have attached to, in order to stop them from spreading throughout the body.

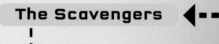

Defender Cells

↓

Lymphocyte

Lymphocytes produce antibodies when they come into contact with a harmful cell. Antibodies are proteins that destroy invading foreign cells.

Attack Cells

↓

Neutrophil

Neutrophil cells patrol the bloodstream and 'eat' any attacking organisms. Once the neutrophil has deactivated the intruder, it will also die, making the infected area safe.

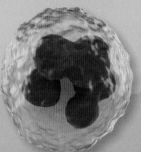

The Commander

⇢

Eosinophil

Eosinophils are in charge! They regulate the body's response to parasites and allergens. When they meet invading organisms, they release chemicals that destroy the virus.

Virus Outbreak Notice

THE AGENCY OF HEALTH PROTECTION is urging citizens to take steps in order to prevent a further outbreak of a new airborne virus that has been sweeping the nation. The disease contains an allergen that can cause an eczema-like rash if it comes into contact with human skin. An official effort to minimise the spread of the virus has been ordered.

How is the virus spread?

▲ The virus is spread from one person to the next in a similar way to the common cold.

▲ The virus is carried within the respiratory system and is transferred by tiny droplets of mucus (snot).

What are the symptoms?

▲ Itchy red rashes appear on the skin. The rash starts in a small area and then will spread if not treated.

What should I do if I think I have contracted the virus?

▲ If the rash does not disappear after three days, seek advice from your doctor, who will be able to prescribe an ointment to soothe the affected area.

Five Steps to Reduce Risk

**Please take the following steps in order to keep
yourself and those close to you at minimal risk:**

1 Avoid contact with those who could be infected.
If you think you have contracted the virus yourself,
then stay at home until symptoms have been gone
for at least 24 hours.

2 Wash your hands after covering your nose and
mouth when sneezing.

3 Clean surfaces regularly as germs can also spread
this way. Computer keyboards, phones, doorknobs
and pens can also hold germs.

4 Stay strong and healthy. Get plenty of sleep and
eat lots of fruit and vegetables. This will help to
keep your immune system in good condition.

5 Avoid touching your face, especially your eyes,
nose and mouth, after touching surfaces in
a public area.

History of Medical Pioneers

2600 BCE Chinese emperor **Huang Ti** lays down the basic principles of Chinese medicine.

1543 Flemish doctor **Andreas Vesalius** publishes the first accurate description of the human anatomy in his book *On the Structure of the Human Body*.

1818 British doctor **James Blundell** performs the first successful transfusion of human blood to a human patient.

2000 BCE   **1500**   **1700**   **1800**

1796 British doctor **Edward Jenner** performs a vaccination against smallpox by inoculating a child with a vaccine containing the weaker cowpox virus.

1846 American dentist **William Morton** uses ether as a general anaesthetic to make a patient unconscious and pain-free during an operation.

It has taken humans thousands of years to learn how to combat diseases. Each breakthrough has helped save lives, and new treatments are still being discovered today.

1895 German physicist **Wilhelm Roentgen** discovers X-rays.

1928 British doctor **Alexander Fleming** discovers penicillin, a substance released by mould that kills bacteria. It will later become the first antibiotic.

1965 British scientist **Harold Hopkins** produces a sophisticated endoscope that gives doctors a clear view of tissues inside the body.

1900

1898 French physicists **Marie** and **Pierre Curie** discover the radioactive element radium, later used in the treatment of cancers.

1967 South African surgeon **Christiaan Barnard** carries out the first successful heart transplant.

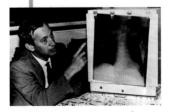

Chapter 5
Scaling the Skeletal System

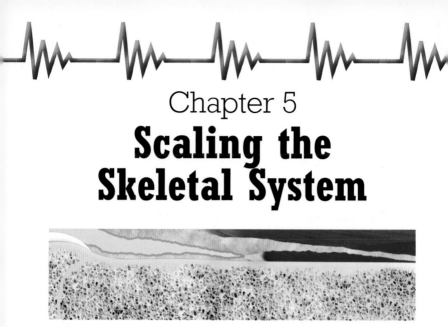

White spindles criss-crossed throughout the entire area around them, overlapping and intersecting. A complex, honeycomb structure connected every part of the solid walls to each other. The walls and pillarlike spindles were a grey-white colour, which slightly reflected a far-off red mass.

"Ah! Oh! Oh dear," Frank sighed. "I'm afraid that... well... we might have gone from bad to even worse."

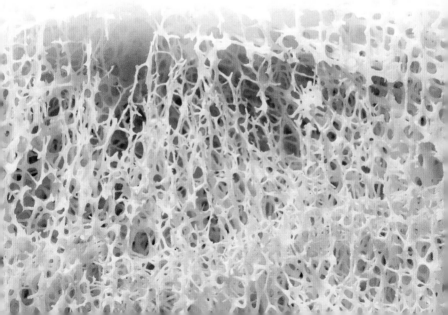

"Worse?" Dan said. "How could this be worse? We're outside the bloodstream. That makes it much better."

"Well yes, that's true, but you see, we're inside a bone." Frank began to move the drone forward slowly. "All these spindles around us are actually the spongy insides at the centre of our bones. These allow the bones to be hollow, while still extra strong."

"That doesn't sound so bad," said Maya.

"Not until you understand why they are hollow." Frank paused dramatically.

"The insides of our bones are filled with soft tissue called bone marrow," Frank continued. "Bone marrow has two colours: red and yellow." He stopped the drone just behind one of the spindles, as if hiding. "Yellow bone marrow stores fat. Do either of you know what the red type does?"

They shook their heads.

Frank moved the drone out from behind the spindle, allowing them to see the marrow below. They saw now why it had looked so red from afar. The large canal of thick liquid was crowded with red blood cells, and as some floated up and out towards the large veins above, more took their place behind... and more... and still more. It seemed endless.

"Red bone marrow creates blood. One of the many jobs of bones, besides supporting our weight and keeping us protected, is to house our blood factories. If they make red blood cells, what do you think they also make?"

Dan and Maya paled. "White blood cells...?"

"Correct! Do you know what else bones are famous for? Being extremely tough. So we can't cut our way out. A vein wall and a bone wall are quite different. So I'm afraid our only way out is back the way we came – back into the bloodstream."

Dan moaned. "But if we go into that huge tube, the white cells will catch us for sure!"

"We came in through a tiny tube," said Maya, "so surely there must be more capillaries in here that we can use? There weren't anywhere near as many white blood cells in those!"

"Hmm, that's not a bad idea, Maya...." Frank sounded thoughtful. "The only problem is we don't know whereabouts in the body we are. All that running away made me lose track of our position, so we don't know what's nearby this particular bone. We can't tell where we might end up until it's too late."

"It's still better than being surrounded by bone marrow," said Dan. "We'll get caught for sure if we stay here."

"True! That settles it then. We'll have to take a chance." Frank took a deep breath. "Keep your eyes peeled. We're going to have to make a dash for it over to the other side. We don't want to end up in the same stream as those angry white blood cells near the liver."

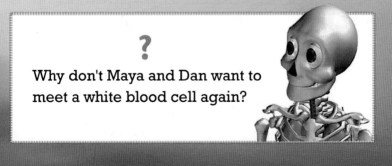

?

Why don't Maya and Dan want to meet a white blood cell again?

The drone zipped from spindle to spindle, Frank hiding behind each one before making another rush to the next. The blood cells swarmed below – thousands of them being produced every second.

They'd almost reached the other side when Maya cried, "Frank, look out!"

The drone swung to a stop behind a spindle just in time for one of the white blood cells to pass, floating farther out than the others, patrolling for anything amiss. They couldn't help but hold their breath as it drifted past. Finally it was far enough from them that Frank could make a dash farther away, and as they reached the other side, it didn't seem to notice. They breathed out.

"Phew... that was too close... nice job, Maya," said Dan. "Can we get out of here now?"

"Definitely," said Frank. "Any capillary will do. Let's get going!"

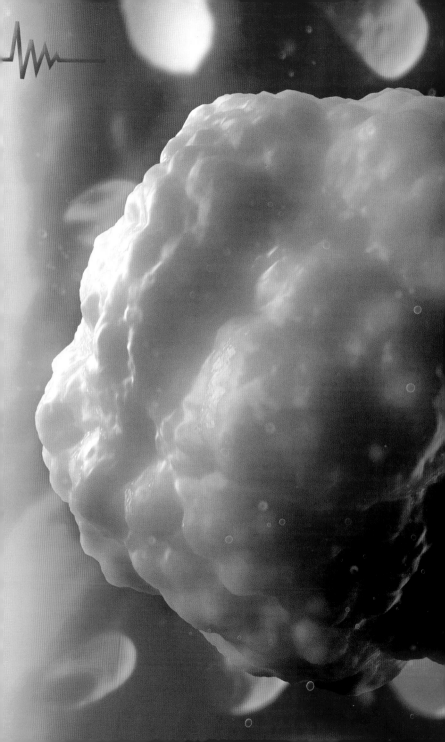

Blood Factory

Red blood cells are worn out after about 120 days so the body is in need of a constant supply of new ones. Millions of new cells enter the bloodstream from the bone marrow every minute.

1 The kidneys send out signals to the red bone marrow telling it to start the cogs turning and make new red blood cells.

2 The machine starts to whir and the production line starts.

Here is how red bone marrow creates new blood cells.

Blood cell production line

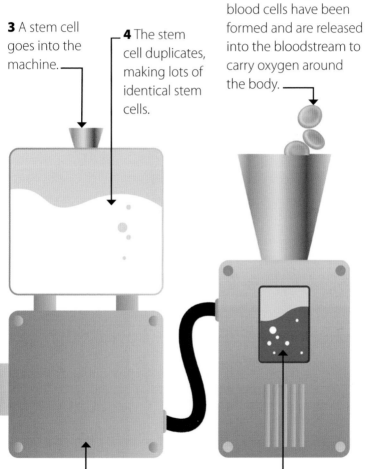

3 A stem cell goes into the machine.

4 The stem cell duplicates, making lots of identical stem cells.

7 After two days, the red blood cells have been formed and are released into the bloodstream to carry oxygen around the body.

5 The stem cells shrink.

6 The stem cells change shape and become dented in the centre.

Skeleton Dance

The following song is based on an old spiritual song *Dem Bones* by the songwriter James Weldon Johnson (1871–1938). Dance along as you say or sing the words, pointing to the various bones.

The toe bone's connected to the foot bone,
The foot bone's connected to the ankle bone,
The ankle bone's connected to the leg bone,
Let's shake those bones about!
The leg bone's connected to the knee bone,
The knee bone's connected to the thigh bone,
The thigh bone's connected to the hip bone,
Let's shake those bones about!
The hip bone's connected to the back bone
The back bone's connected to the neck bone,
The neck bone's connected to the head bone,
Let's shake those bones about!
Them bones, them bones, them dry bones.
Them bones, them bones, them dry bones.
Them bones, them bones, them dry bones.
Let's shake those bones about!

The song used the simple bone names. However each bone also has a scientific name.

Skull

Cervical vertebrae

Lumbar vertebrae

Pelvic girdle

Femur

Fibula

Tibia

Tarsals

Metatarsals

89

"Doctor, Doctor" Jokes

"Doctor, Doctor" jokes have been around for hundreds of years. Some researchers found some in the world's oldest surviving joke book from the third century. So they date back to at least ancient Roman times.

Doctor, Doctor, I've broken my arm in two places.

Well, don't go back there again then!

Doctor, Doctor, you have to help me out!

Certainly! Which way did you come in?

Doctor, Doctor, I keep thinking there are two of me.

One at a time, please.

Doctor, Doctor, I think I'm a telephone.

Well, take these pills and if they don't work, then give me a ring!

Doctor, Doctor, I've swallowed my pocket money.

Take this and we'll see if there's any change in the morning.

Doctor, Doctor, I feel like a pair of curtains.

Well, pull yourself together then.

Doctor, Doctor, I dream there are monsters under my bed. What can I do?

Saw the legs off your bed!

Doctor, Doctor, I think I'm a bridge.

What's come over you?

Oh! Two cars, a large truck and a coach.

Doctor, Doctor, I'm becoming invisible.

Yes, I can see you're not all there!

Doctor, Doctor, I keep thinking I'm a caterpillar.

Don't worry! You'll soon change!

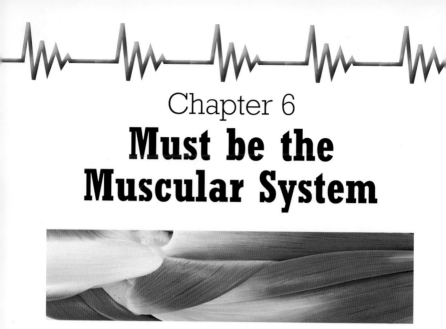

Chapter 6
Must be the Muscular System

Back in the bloodstream at last, Dan and Maya looked ahead to find themselves drifting through a tiny tunnel with uncountable alleys and offshoots of other blood vessels all around them. They tried to see farther ahead, but for the first time, the tunnel around them was moving!

"Where are we?" asked Maya. "That straight bit ahead just turned into a corner. They've never moved before!"

"Are they floating?" Dan wondered aloud, as the way ahead moved in a repeating, bulging motion. "It's like we're rocking on the sea or something."

"Ah, not at all!" Frank sounded excited again. "This makes perfect sense. Do you know what surrounds almost every bone in the body?"

The pair thought back to their project.

"Hmm… muscles?" ventured Maya.

"Exactly right! And muscles move all the time, even in just tiny ways we don't even notice. The veins around them need to move with them, which means we're next to, or perhaps travelling through, a muscle."

"A muscle?" Maya paused. "Do we know which one? Maybe we can figure out where we are that way."

"Not likely," said Dan. "During our project, I read there were more than six hundred muscles. We could be in any of them!"

"There are six hundred and forty around the skeleton alone," Frank said, "but most of those muscles don't work alone. They work together in groups to pull different ways and allow your body to carefully adjust your position. Each one can only move one way, you see, so they need to work as a team."

Dan frowned. "But I can move my arms in lots of different ways, like when you move your arms up and down. That's two ways!"

"Ah, yes! However," said Frank grandly, "muscles can only contract! They just all do it in different directions. So when one pulls your arm up for you, and you want to lower it, another one pulls it back again. A bit like a seesaw! If you sit on one end, you can't make your side go up, but if you work with someone on the other end—"

"You can make each other go up and down," finished Maya. "I never realised that."

"Fascinating, isn't it?" Frank grinned. "Since they need to be so flexible, so do their blood vessels, and anything else connected to them. You wouldn't want to lose blood because your muscle cut it off by moving."

"They must need to be able to stretch, too," added Dan, looking down one of the passing alleys. "My dad lifts heavy things and has large muscles. I guess the blood doesn't get cut off even when they grow big like his."

"Definitely not!" said Frank. "Oxygen is extremely important for muscles, so they need blood to get it to them at all times. And, should you ever want to exercise your muscles, knowing how they work will help."

"Really? Why?"

"Because," Frank said, "when you strain a muscle more than it's used to, the muscle can tear."

"What!" Dan sounded horrified.

"You can tear your muscles?"

"Yes indeed," Frank replied. "Thankfully your body is very adaptive. If you tear your muscles, your body will repair them, but – and this is amazing – it will repair them to be stronger than before."

"How?" asked Maya. "Just by making them bigger?"

"Sort of, yes!" said Frank. "Muscles are made of hundreds of thousands of tiny fibres, all wrapped up together like a bale of hay. So when a muscle is used a lot, the old fibres are repaired and some more muscle fibres are wrapped around the damage to make that particular place stronger. Your body wants to make you as durable as you need to be. If you're doing a lot of the same activity, like a runner training for the Olympics, the muscles you are using are made stronger so you can do it more easily."

"That's amazing!" said Maya. "How could our bodies know how to do that?"

"Hmm, I wonder...," said Frank. "There should be a way to show you nearby...."
He floated the drone along until he randomly stopped, and declared, "Yes, here!"

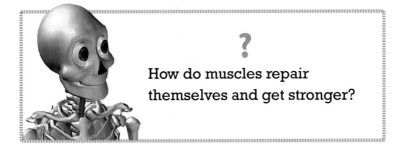

He cut a hole in the wall of the blood vessel, and inside was a small bundle of tubes. Dan thought they were about the size of drain pipes, until he realised that this was in comparison to the drone. These tubes must really be extra tiny.

?

How do muscles repair themselves and get stronger?

"This bundle is made of nerve endings."
Frank sounded particularly happy with
himself for finding it. "There's a little bundle
in each muscle, acting like an on-and-off
switch. When the brain needs the muscle

to work, it sends a message to this nerve bundle, and it'll contract itself. When the muscle is damaged, the brain will get a message from here, letting it know. It's like its own little two-way radio."

"Wow, it is small for something so important," said Maya.

"All nerve endings are microscopic, since they wind their way through every tiny bit of the body." He paused. "Nerve cells are so small and quick that they can travel from the brain to the big toe in just 0.01 second."

"No way!" Dan and Maya both exclaimed, but their surprise was cut short as the red blood cells around them started bobbing out of the way, creating a path to them. They all turned to look down the tube to see why. What they saw coming towards them at full speed, was a single white blood cell.

Muscle Machine

All muscles in the human body have to work together to keep us on the move. Even the smallest muscles have their own part to play.

Components

About 640 muscles cover a human skeleton. Most are connected to the bones with stretchy straps of tendons.

Smooth muscle forms part of organs. These muscles are made of long, thin fibres and are mostly linked together in muscular sheets.

Hip muscles

Quadriceps

Hamstring muscle

Wow!
The fastest muscles are in your eyeballs, shifting your gaze in 0.02 of a second!

Triceps

Neck muscle

Jaw muscles

Biceps

Function

■ Skeletal muscles shrink and shorten to pull tight and move bones. You can purposely control these via neurons in the nerves from your brain.

Main features

■ The biggest muscles pull your legs straight at the hip.

■ The smallest muscles are inside your ear.

■ There are more than 14 muscles in your tongue.

■ Calf muscles pull your heels so you can walk, run or stand on tiptoe.

Funny Faces

This diagram shows some of the main muscles that make facial expressions.

There are more than 40 muscles in your face that can make over 7,000 different expressions. A slight muscle pull can make tiny, precise movements of the facial skin.

Flat forehead muscle raises the eyebrow and wrinkles the forehead.

Circular eye muscle helps close the eyelid.

Cheek muscle pulls corner of the mouth upwards and outwards.

Mouth muscle brings lips together and helps shape words when speaking.

Jaw muscle pulls corner of mouth outwards.

Lower jaw muscle pulls corner of mouth downwards.

How many funny faces can you make? Which muscles are you moving?

Clench test

1 Hold your hand above your head and clench and unclench your fist. Count how many times you can clench it before it starts feeling uncomfortable.

2 Now do the same with your other hand, but this time hold it down by your side. How many times can you clench before this feels uncomfortable?

Relax test

Clasp your hands together with the fingers interlocked. Stretch out your index fingers straight and parallel to each other so they are not touching.

What happens to your index fingers when you let your arm muscles relax?

Explanation of test results

You should manage more clenches with your hand held by your side. This is because blood flows more quickly downwards than upwards, so the oxygen supply reaches the muscles quicker.

Your fingers should move towards each other as they relax. This is because skeletal muscles return to a relaxed position when not active.

105

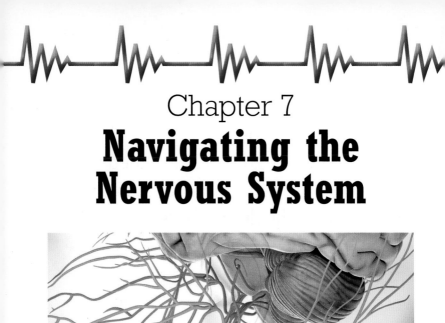

Chapter 7
Navigating the Nervous System

"Oh no! The white blood cell is coming for us!" cried Maya.

"I… I don't think we can outrun this one, kids. I'm sorry," Frank said.

"What?" Dan flailed in panic. "But it'll eat us! We have to get away. Let's go, quickly."

"It's too fast, and we're not even moving." Frank turned the drone back to the bundle of nerves nestled into the muscle. "Even if we run, by the time we get going, it'll have caught up with us." Despite his words, he didn't sound defeated. "But we've had

106

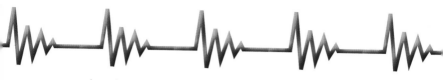

a good adventure, haven't we? So how about one last ride before it's all over?"

"How can we? It's nearly here!" cried Dan.

"I'm going to open the nerve, push the camera part of the drone inside, and when the white blood cell crashes into us, it'll fire you right up the tube." Frank made a 'whoosh' sound. "We've never seen inside a nerve before. They're normally too small, so how about we give it a try?"

Despite the incoming cell, he sounded excited. The pair paused. Frank's excitement was infectious. They nodded together. "Let's do it!"

Frank worked quickly, and as he pushed the camera inside, they couldn't see how close the white cell was. "Wait for it...," said Frank. "Now!"

The camera suddenly shot up the tube, blown off the front of the drone by the force behind. They were dazzled by the sparks and bright glowing specks that rushed past them in all directions, confused by everything they could see. It took them a few moments, but finally they started making sense of things – their direction, the tube they were in and their speed. And what speed! They were moving faster than the drone had ever been able to. Frank's voice filtered into their ears.

"My goodness! What a sight! Quite

incredible, isn't it?"

"Yes!" Maya didn't know where to look.
"I'm not even sure what anything is."

"Well, it's hard to spot anything exactly because you're moving so fast," said Frank. The sheer speed made them almost want to shout, even though they couldn't hear through the camera. "I think you're being carried along by the electricity in the nerves, so all those sparks and lights you see are probably connections being made around the body."

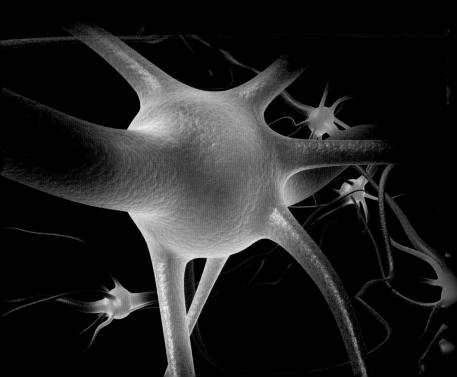

"Electricity?" Dan stared. "We have electricity in our bodies?"

"More than you'd think, Dan," said Frank. "The nervous system is like our bodies' wiring. The brain sends signals to every part of the body at once, telling which systems to operate and when, with intricate details."

"That makes the whole body like some kind of computer," said Dan. "That's amazing!"

"Yes it is! But if the body is like a computer, then it's one of the most powerful in existence. Even in this modern day, we're still catching up with nature." Frank watched as they sped up faster and faster, shooting through the system of nerves. "Can you imagine, the brain alone has over a hundred billion nerve cells in it. The rest of the body has an uncountable number. So, you see, our bodies truly are a fascinating system."

The picture started to become crackly and unclear. Instead of the twists and turns of the thousands of nerves before, they now flew along one single tunnel, racing up towards the end.

"We must be in the central nervous system now, travelling along the spine," said Frank. "The picture isn't so clear anymore. I think there are just too many signals rushing past. We're struggling to receive just one. I doubt we'll be able to see anything once we reach the brain… that's the hub of everything, and the body will just dispose of the camera safely."

Maya and Dan watched in awe as they travelled up the spine. The bright flashes of electrical signals connecting and becoming so numerous, they were almost unable to see where they were heading. As the lights intensified, the picture on the screens became even more fuzzy. Finally they

reached
the end of
the spine
where, for a split
second, they saw a vast
network ahead of them, so
immense they could barely
imagine how much activity
was happening every second.
For that split second, they saw
the brain.

Grey Matters

Using Your Head

The brain is made from cells that do all of your thinking and feeling. Different areas of the brain control different bodily functions including thinking, moving, feeling and memory.

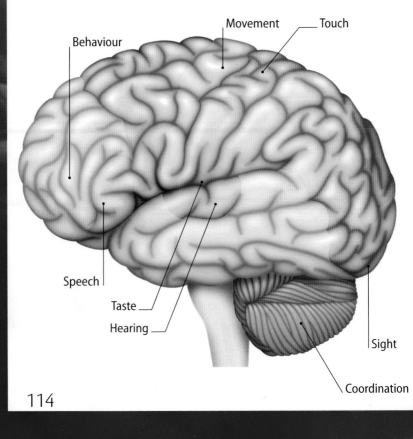

Behaviour

Movement

Touch

Speech

Taste

Hearing

Sight

Coordination

Why do we need a brain?

Here are examples of just some of the activities that we need our brain for.

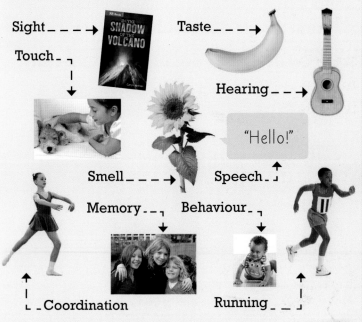

Sight - - - →
Touch
Taste - - - →
Hearing - - →
"Hello!"
Smell - - - →
Speech
Memory
Behaviour
Coordination
Running

Wow! Did you know?

1. Flattened out, your brain would cover an ironing board.

2. Your brain generates as much energy as a small lightbulb even when you're sleeping.

3. The human brain is over three times as big as the brain of other mammals that are of a similar body size.

4. The brain of an adult human weighs around 1.5 kg (3 lbs). Although it makes up just 2% of the body's weight, it uses around 20% of its energy.

Are You a Genius?

An IQ (intelligence quotient) test measures intelligence but this can mean many different things. Discover which aspect you are best at by taking this genius test.

Spatial intelligence

1. Which shape completes the sentence?

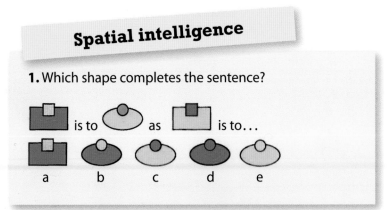

is to ⬭ as ⬓ is to...

a b c d e

Verbal intelligence

2. Which word doesn't belong?
a) shout
b) sing
c) talk
d) walk
e) whisper

Numerical intelligence

3. 1985516 is to sheep as 2315126 is to
a) wolf
b) horse
c) antelope
d) goat
e) cattle

Hint:
a=1, b=2, c=3... z=26

Lateral thinking

4. It's spring. You see a carrot and two pieces of coal together in somebody's front garden. How did they get there?

5. A man lives on the tenth floor of a building. Every day he takes the lift to the ground floor to go to work. When he returns, he takes the lift to the seventh floor and walks the rest of the way. If it's raining, he takes the lift all the way up. Why?
Clue: *he owns an umbrella.*

Answers
1 b; **2** d; **3** a; **4** They were part of a snowman's face in winter, but the snowman melted; **5** The man is short and can't reach higher than button 7 in the lift. On rainy days, he carries an umbrella and can use it to push the top button.

117

Navigating the Nervous System

TOP SECRET MISSION

Your mission, Agent Neuron, should you choose to accept it, is to deliver a top-secret message to the right hand in a split second. Our superiors in the brain have informed us that this hand has touched something hot. We need to move this hand away from the heat as soon as possible in order to eliminate any risk to our human. A map of the nervous system showing the brain, spinal cord and all the nerves is pictured here; this specifies the route you need to take. Beware of any danger along the way and good luck, Agent Neuron! We're counting on you.

Nerves
THE ROUTE NETWORK
Bundles of fibres that spread all over the body. These carry signals between the brain and other parts of the body.

Neuron
THE AGENT
One of billions of nerve cells that use electrical and chemical signals to process and send information, telling the body what to do, for example, move a finger.

Brain
THE CONTROL CENTRE
A web of thick wrinkles of folded tissue where instructions are received, interpreted and sent out.

Nervous system map

This system regulates almost every bodily process, from breathing to controlling reactions when feeling physical pain.

Key:

AGENT NEURON'S JOURNEY

Begin in the brain, travel down the spine, and then along to the right hand.

Epilogue
A World Inside Us All

Maya and Dan removed their helmets and were once again back inside the lab. Frank stood in his bright white lab coat, hands clasped in front of him, with a wide grin on his face. Mary sat calmly in her chair, with a book in her hand. She looked up and smiled. They were staring at her.

"That… all that…," Dan began, "it was all inside you!"

"Well, yes!" Mary nodded. "But it's all inside you, too. It's inside every one of us."

Maya looked at Dan, Frank and then

Mary, before finally down at herself. She examined her hand, imagining the blood cells, the bones all connected, the network of nerves running throughout, all working together. "Wow!" she said quietly.

A Trip Through the Body Quiz

See if you can remember the answers to these questions about what you have read.

1. What is an endoscope?

2. What makes blood red?

3. What is the function of white blood cells?

4. Why does Maya's brother find it difficult to breathe?

5. How does the body stop food from going into the windpipe?

6. What are the feelers in the small intestine connected to?

7. Where in the body would you expect to find proteases?

8. After visiting the liver, how do Dan, Maya and Frank escape the white blood cells chasing them?

9. Who carried out the first successful heart transplant?

10. Why was Frank worried when he realised that the drone was in Mary's bone marrow?

11. What type of cells are blood cells made from?

12. How does a muscle know when it needs to contract?

13. According to Frank, approximately how many nerve cells are in an average human brain?

14. Why had Frank not seen inside a nerve before?

15. What carried the camera along Mary's nerves?

Answers on page 125.

Glossary

Antibody
Substance made by the body that sticks to germs and marks them for destruction by white blood cells.

Artery
Blood vessel that carries blood away from the heart to the body's tissues and organs.

Blood vessel
Tube that carries blood through the body.

Capillary
The smallest type of blood vessel.

Cells
The smallest living units that are the building blocks of the human body.

Digestion
The process that breaks down food into tiny particles that your body can absorb and use.

Haemoglobin
Substance that carries oxygen in red blood cells.

Immune system
Collection of cells and tissues that protect the body from disease by searching for and destroying germs.

Nerve
Cablelike bundle of neurons that links all body parts to the brain and spinal cord.

Neuron
Nerve cell that carries information around the body as electrical signals.

Organ
Major body part that has a specific function.

Plasma
The liquid, colourless part of the blood.

Vein
Blood vessel that carries blood towards the heart.

Index

Answers to A Trip Through the Body Quiz:

1. A small instrument, often a camera, which doctors use to look inside patients' bodies; **2.** Haemoglobin – a red-coloured protein contained in red blood cells; **3.** Patrol the bloodstream and fight off diseases and infections; **4.** Because he has asthma; **5.** The epiglottis moves to cover the windpipe when we eat; **6.** The bloodstream; **7.** In the stomach; **8.** They cut their way out of a capillary and a platelet closes up the gap; **9.** Christiaan Barnard; **10.** Because bone marrow makes white blood cells; **11.** Stem cells; **12.** The brain sends a message to the nerve cells in the muscle; **13.** 100 billion; **14.** Because nerves are too small; **15.** Electricity.

Guide for Parents

DK Reads is a three-level interactive reading adventure series for children, developing the habit of reading widely for both pleasure and information. These chapter books have an exciting main narrative interspersed with a range of reading genres to suit your child's reading ability, as required by the National Curriculum. Each book is designed to develop your child's reading skills, fluency, grammar awareness, and comprehension in order to build confidence and engagement when reading.

Ready for a *Reading Alone* book

YOUR CHILD SHOULD

- be able to read independently and silently for extended periods of time.
- read aloud flexibly and fluently, in expressive phrases with the listener in mind.
- respond to what they are reading with an enquiring mind.

A VALUABLE AND SHARED READING EXPERIENCE

Supporting children when they are reading proficiently can encourage them to value reading and to view reading as an interesting, purposeful and enjoyable pastime. So here are a few tips on how to use this book with your child.

TIP 1 Reading aloud as a learning opportunity:

- if your child has already read some of the book, ask him/her to explain the earlier part briefly.
- encourage your child to read slightly slower than his/her normal silent reading speed so that the words are clear and the listener has time to absorb the information, too.

Reading aloud provides your child with practice in expressive reading and performing to a listener, as well as a chance to share his/her responses to the storyline and the information.

TIP 2 Praise, share and chat:

- encourage your child to recall specific details after each chapter.
- provide opportunities for your child to pick out interesting words and discuss what they mean.
- discuss how the author captures the reader's interest, or how effective the non-fiction layouts are.
- ask the questions provided on some pages and in the quiz. These help to develop comprehension skills and awareness of the language used.
- ask if there's anything that your child would like to discover more about.

Further information can be researched in the index of other non-fiction books or on the Internet.

A FEW ADDITIONAL TIPS

- Continue to read to your child regularly to demonstrate fluency, phrasing and expression; to find out or check information; and for sharing enjoyment.
- Encourage your child to read a range of different genres, such as newspapers, poems, review articles and instructions.
- Provide opportunities for your child to read to a variety of eager listeners, such as a sibling or a grandparent.

Series consultant **Shirley Bickler** is a longtime advocate of carefully crafted, enthralling texts for young readers. Her LIFT initiative for infant teaching was the model for the National Literacy Strategy Literacy Hour, and she is co-author of *Book Bands for Guided Reading* published by Reading Recovery based at the Institute of Education.

Have you read these other great books from DK?

READING ALONE

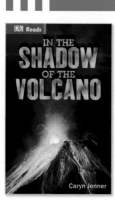

Dramatic modern-
day adventure as
Mount Vesuvius
re-awakens.

Life-or-death
futuristic space
adventure to find a
new home planet.

Pulse-racing
action adventure
chasing twisters in
Tornado Alley.

Time-travelling
adventure caught
up in the intrigue
in ancient Rome.

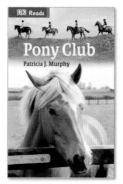

Emma adores
horses. Will her
wish come true at
a riding camp?

Lucy follows her
dream to train as
a professional
dancer.